T0118300

Linda: Our Eyes and Her Soul

Laugh, Linda, Laugh, and Bring the Face of God to You

Joseph Andrejchak Galata

iUniverse, Inc.
New York   Bloomington

Linda: Our Eyes and Her Soul
Laugh, Linda, Laugh, and Bring the Face of God to You

Copyright © 2009 by Joseph Andrejchak Galata.

All rights reserved. No part of this book may be used or reproduced by any means, graphic, electronic, or mechanical, including photocopying, recording, taping or by any information storage retrieval system without the written permission of the publisher except in the case of brief quotations embodied in critical articles and reviews.

The views expressed in this work are solely those of the author and do not necessarily reflect the views of the publisher, and the publisher hereby disclaims any responsibility for them.

iUniverse books may be ordered through booksellers or by contacting:

iUniverse
1663 Liberty Drive
Bloomington, IN 47403
www.iuniverse.com
1-800-Authors (1-800-288-4677)

Because of the dynamic nature of the Internet, any Web addresses or links contained in this book may have changed since publication and may no longer be valid.

Photographs reproduced by Shayda Galata Photography

ISBN: 978-1-4401-3944-4 (pbk)
ISBN: 978-1-4401-3945-1 (ebk)

Printed in the United States of America

iUniverse rev. date: 4/23/2009

Also by Joseph Galata

Theatrical Productions, Publications, Media Programs, and Workshops/Seminars

on the theme

"Healing From Grief"

I Will Hire You As A Minstrel

My Grandmother's Dance

I Dance For My Dying Son

Rumi: Grief To Ecstasy

On The Flip Side

Dance O Dervish Dance

Frozen Plums of Mitar Tarabic

Dark Night Of The Soul

Diamonds For A Glass Of Water

Footsteps Of Children Left Behind

Little Mary Ellen

Giacomo Leopardi

The Ghost of the Frozen Plum Tree Farmer

These Happy Memories Bring Sweet Tears of Ache

The Final Is Never The Final

For Linda

Everyone has an assigned destiny.

Yours was to show us how to laugh.

"This was a solemn day; now from amusements

You seek repose; and in a dream perhaps

You will recall how many hearts you pleased today,

How many, too, pleased you."

Giacomo Leopardi

"La sera del di di festa" (The Evening after the Holiday)

1820

Contents

Acknowledgments

I am indebted to the atoms of my ancestors that dance and spiral within my cells. It is their astonishing force of energy flowing and swirling within the precise and absolute beauty of nature that gives me comfort in mourning. Through their echoing, existing beyond time, I am gifted with the creativity to write the following pages.

Preface

"We watched her breathing thro' the night,

Her breathing soft and low,

As in her breast the wave of life,

Kept heaving to and fro.

So silently we seem'd to speak,

So slowly mov'd about,

As we had lent her half our powers

To eek her living out.

Our very hopes belied our fears,

Our fears our hopes belied,

We thought her dying when she slept,

And sleeping when she died.

For when the morn came dim and sad,

And chill with early showers,

Her quiet eyelids clos'd- she had,

Another morn than ours.

Thomas Hood (1799-1845) "The Death-Bed"

When not face-to-face with grief, we live within the most joyful moments generated by life's interactions. During good times, we unleash our hidden creative powers as appreciation of the exquisite craftsmanship of either mysterious or mystical forces that inhabits our very cells. Yet, we find it distasteful and confusing when forced to acknowledge that life comes with risks. When it comes to the end-of-life journey, dying and death offer no guarantee to please.

As a child, I lived across the street from the Grandview Cemetery. I sat on the wooden porch with my maternal grandfather, a legless amputee, watching funerals and listening to his ghost stories. When Grandpa died, I became afraid of both dying and being dead. As a Slavic Roman Catholic child, I began praying to St. Joseph, the patron saint for a happy death. Later, when I was nine years old, sitting on the porch of an impoverished home in a small community along the river, I watched with fascination the neighborhood men carrying the body of "old Elmer the barber" out of his house, down the hill, through our backyard which was the community junkyard, and into someone's car. I said to myself, "No wonder he suddenly fell over dead while giving his wife Ethel a haircut, he was a Methodist and couldn't pray to St. Joseph." That year I asked my paternal grandmother, Mary Andrejchak Galata, a staunch Catholic, to buy me a specific present for my birthday; a St. Joseph medal to wear around my neck. Paranoid about dying and being dead, I wore that necklace for the next eight years. A few days after I graduated from high school, I decided to toss caution to the wind, tempt God, and challenge St. Joseph. I put the holy medal inside a cardboard box filled with my treasured adolescent memorabilia, and I moved away from McKeesport, Pennsylvania.

I left home when I was 17 years old because I had a deep-seated spiritual, artistic, social, and theological need to investigate, access, and embrace various cultural perceptions of life's reality, including dying and death. My self-imposed "place myself in the hands of fate journey" with energetic geographical leaps, took me through international nooks and crannies of ethnological, religious, folkloric, theatrical, and literary cultural populations. Yet, decades later, even having grown older and multifarious about the meaning of life, dying and death continues to be an enigma.

Whether it was the perishing of a parent, four grandparents, numerous friends and peers in my professional communities of education, arts, media, social services, and hospice, I have struggled to increase, change, grasp and solidify my perception of life's reality by searching for both meaning and truth in all the euphemisms for dying: passing away, moving on, making the transition, a new journey, starting over, returning home, rest in peace.

But as experience has revealed to me, in the death of a loved one I learn that how I create, nurture, strengthen, direct and control the energy of my thoughts, emotions, and actions, will eventually resolve, shape, and form the manner and quality of my dying and death.

Towards this desire to understand dying and death, I cannot overstate that specific theories and works of art shine a light; the atomic structure of the soul and the origin of consciousness as proposed by the ancient Greek philosopher Lucretius, the aesthetic theology of higher consciousness as proclaimed by19th century Russian Orthodox scientist and writer Pavel Florensky, the spiritual centrality demonstrated by the Catholic Pope John XX111, the mystical experiences of life after death as shared by the Swedish visionary Emmanuel Swedenborg, the sense of spiritual expansion as expressed in the stanzas composed by the Turkish, Afghani, and Persian Sufis Rumi, Hafez, and Hallaj, the desire to search for compassionate beauty as encouraged by the Italian poet Giacomo Leopardi, the 19th century prophecies of the Serbian plum tree farmer Mitar Tarabich, and the epitome of finding meaningfulness with social contributions as exemplified by Mr. Charles Dickens of Victorian England, have enriched my ability to speak, write, and counsel about dying, death, and healing from grief.

But until my sister Linda's death in July 2008, I did not feel I had deep wisdom about dying and death, only many personal and professional experiences to interpret and share with audiences, students, and clients. Linda's unexpected dying and death has made my personal and professional work in bereavement far more graceful, fierce, gentle and intense than ever.

As her eldest brother I witnessed her childhood and adolescent pain caused by the unnecessary social ridicules, taunts, and mockeries by both peers and strangers. But since adolescence, I believed that the buoyant spirit of my mentally delayed-disabled sister hovered for 54 years between earth and heaven, and that her soul was influenced by the tranquil energies of angels and ancestors with incandescent brilliancy.

My sister Linda was mentally-retarded but not spiritually-retarded.

She bore, in my eyes, the same characteristics of love, pathos, and forgiveness as the Catholic saints I had read about in the catechism books. I was 13 years old when I first had the thought, "Linda doesn't know how to hate!"

At the age of 54 when she was unexpectedly on her death bed inside the Westmoreland Hospital in Greensburg, Pennsylvania, her family members, especially her husband of 33 years, a mentally disabled-delayed man with flaming red hair and matching moustache, realized how precious Linda was to so many people as a teacher of laughter, joy, appreciation, love, and perhaps more than any other virtue, forgiveness.

The following pages are not about the vicissitudes which afflicted Linda's life since her birth on April 24, 1954 in McKeesport, Pennsylvania. Nor is this story about the love of her life following her autumn wedding to Nelson Heckman. This book is about changes Linda went through during her final days on earth and the beginning moments of her spirit's ascension into the Heavens of Pre-Existence.

For days, her dying was witnessed by the weary eyes of family members. Siblings were losing a sister, a mother was being robbed of a daughter, and a mentally disabled-delayed husband was suffering from a broken heart. As Linda lay sound asleep and others were wide awake in perplexity, confusion, and fear, heaven seemed far away from all of us who were mourning.

But so often lost in thought, I imagined that Linda's innocent mind, beautiful spirit, and radiant soul were being greeted by the translucent energies of majestic angels and colorful ancestors. While we privately grieved and publicly mourned, I believe that Linda's essence was penetrating the veil between the visible and invisible worlds as she ascended into the multi-colored atoms swirling within the secret chambers of heaven.

A few hours before Linda's spirit passed into a realm where sorrow is no longer, I was 3,625 miles away, spinning and stomping in a spiritual ritual I inherited from my ancient ancestors who danced as prayer to worship God, honor ancestors, express gratitude, supplicate needs, and fulfill an assigned destiny. While spinning to the rhythm of the music, I chanted the Middle Eastern supplication "Dance, O Dervish, Dance and bring the Face of God to me." I was not paying attention to the technical merits of the dancing since my thoughts and prayers were with my sister. I was picturing in my mind the beautiful memories I had as I knew her throughout her infancy, childhood, adolescence, and adulthood. Suddenly, when the music hit a crescendo of Eastern European notes, there was a feeling that I was being summoned to witness heavenly joy. Spinning and twirling faster, I had a strange sensation as if I had suddenly received a blessing. I heard Linda's voice whisper into my heart, "Joooeeeeyyyy, I'm not retarded anymore."

At that precise moment, inspired by Linda's strong and vital energy, an idea overtook me. I would write this story about Linda's dying, death, and return to the joyful heavens of our ancestors and guardian angels.

"On earth as it is in heaven"

Laugh, O Linda, Laugh and bring the face of God to you.

Introduction

One day in the autumn of her 21st year, a mentally disabled-delayed girl with an exuberant laugh walked into a vocational rehabilitation center to begin training for a career as an "envelope stuffer". On that fateful day in Greensburg, Pennsylvania, Linda Galata saw Nelson Heckman, a mentally challenged man sitting at his desk across the crowded room. Two days later Linda and Nelson were discovered missing from their respective work stations. The director of the training center discovered the amorous couple in a closet, kissing passionately. Less than a month later after Linda was fired for "disrupting a co-worker's attention to his work," and Nelson was put on cautionary probation for "continuous and unacceptable romantic behavior in the workplace," the disabled man and woman with energetic hearts became husband and wife. For 33 years in a rural western Pennsylvania town, they created their own community of people who loved and helped them. At the Pantalone Funeral Home in July 2009, doctors, nurses, social workers, therapists, bus drivers, donut bakers, shopping mall clerks, and bingo players of diverse religions, races, and ethnic heritages, paid homage to Linda, "who never stopped laughing," "who was the most genuine person," "who made us all laugh," "who loved everyone." As I verbally eulogized at Linda's funeral, "There are people who will say 'Linda had a big heart.' But I think it goes beyond that. For 54 years Linda had an energetic heart which was filled with appreciation, forgiveness, humility, understanding, and valor, spreading love and laughter."

CLOSER TO THE HEAVENS

"You will not long be orphaned in the dark; for from the other side you soon will see the heaven grows white again; the dawn begins, and then the sun returns, which burning brightly with tremendous fire shall flood with shining streams of the light yourself and the ethereal fields."
Giacomo Leopardi

Let us gaze at what is happening in the visible world in a corridor of the third floor inside the Westmoreland Hospital of Greensburg, Pennsylvania.

Standing, sitting, and leaning against the long grayish-white desk stacked with computers, folders, papers, and utensils, in this corridor are nurses, doctors, technicians, and custodians. Writing on medical charts, typing on computers, speaking into stationary and mobile phones, lifting heavy wet mops out of steel buckets and splashing puddles of waters onto the tan linoleum floor, adjusting colorful tubes and metal knobs on an electrical assortment of machines, each person is participating in both soft and loud conversations. A few staff members who are working overtime are munching on kernels of cheese popcorn, chewing on twisted sticks of red licorice, and sipping from pop and water bottles.

Across the slippery floor, two sets of silver elevator doors open and close releasing somber, hesitant, and nervous visitors. Nostrils are flaring and eyes are squinting from stringent fear, worry, and grief, as well as from the strong pungency of multi-scented bouquets of flowers and disinfectant floor bleach.

Inside the various rooms along the long pristine white walled hallway, clusters of restless teenagers and bewildered children are sitting on chairs against bare walls and wishing they could escape to a hockey rink, video arcade, or shopping mall. Uncomfortable middle aged adults are whispering to one another about the vulnerabilities of their own lives and gossiping about the lives of family members who aren't able or aren't brave enough to be in the room. Elderly women share stories, more than a few of them conversing in crisp Slovak, Hungarian, Serbian, and Polish. Old men either dressed in starched Sunday church suits or corduroy hunting pants and plaid shirts are complaining, "those were the days we knew how to work hard," "once our steel mills shut down in this town, nothing's been the same around here," "I've been to this hospital hundreds of times and nobody ever made me spit out my tobacco before, now we got all kinds of stupid rules." The people in the patients' lives, grandfathers, grandmothers, mothers, fathers, brothers and sisters, are scattered about in rooms standing impatiently or seated uncomfortably, most of them staring out windows and wishing they had the power to turn back time. Each person, man, woman, and child in one of the third floor rooms in the Westmoreland Hospital in western Pennsylvania is staring at another person who is lying in a bed within the Intensive Care Unit, and every person is trying to ignore the sudden outbursts of crying coming from the room closest to the desk in the corridor.

In ICU where the intermittent cries originate from, there is a stainless steel breathing machine, a grey oxygen tank with a long green tube, a pink suction machine on a black dolly, tall white IV fluid poles, yellow fluid bags, black cords connected to monitors with green, red, and yellow flicking lights, orange tubes and greenish-blue needles, connecting Linda Galata Heckman to life. The heartbroken man with flaming red hair and matching moustache in the wheelchair, Mr. Nelson Heckman, privately attends to the dying process of his loyal wife and daily companion of thirty-three years. He cannot privately grief for long and screams like a wounded baby which echoes through the 3rd floor.

Lowering the lids over Linda's non-reactive brown eyes and quickly removing his latex exam gloves, a youthful-looking physician in a long white coat covering his turquoise kakis, an honest sadness to his voice, mumbles, "We'll take care of you, Linda."

Linda's mother Jewell, herself a hospital patient because of severe heart pains brought on by anxiety and depression, and Linda's sister Nancy, an exhausted nurse, wife, mother, family caretaker and comforter, are also in Linda's room, stroking the dying sister/daughter's cold face and hands. Each is bending over and smoothing strands of her wet brown hair, whispering into her ear "we're here, Linda," and kissing her forehead in the spirit of love, but also knowing that they will soon be entering the Patalone Funeral Home on West Pittsburgh Avenue and performing the traditional Slavic ritual of kissing their deceased loved one so as to prevent the spirit from roaming throughout eternity searching for the goodbye kisses not received from loved ones.

Linda's entwined hands are resting on the white sheet and holding a card with a secret message written in scribbled penmanship and the signature, *Nelson.* "

Sitting in his wheelchair across the room and feeling the intense rays of the July sun magnified by the closed window pane, staring at the floor and twirling the ends of his red flaming mustache, Nelson is angrily shouting a common refrain to his cries, "Come on, Linda! Wake up and get out of that bed!"

Standing at bedside, the doctor is swiftly straightening the white sheets covering his patient's slowly breathing obese body. Resuming the physical posture and emotional demeanor mandated for demonstrating nuances of professional protocol, the physician turns to Jewell and Nancy whose faces are reflecting utter helplessness.

"I haven't heard from Linda's social worker. Have you talked to him yet?" the physician asks.

Nelson shouts, "He's on vacation. He's coming back today. Why can't you make Linda wake up? You made her better all the other times she was sick!"

"Her organs are shutting down this time, Nelson."

"What can you do, Doctor?" Jewell is asking.

"I got to go wee-wee again! Stupid bladder! The medicine isn't helping me," Nelson shouts from the corner.

"Do you need a nurse to help you go to the bathroom, Nelson?" Nancy asks gently.

"Noooooooooooooo! I know how to pee all by myself, thank you!" the mentally delayed-disabled 55 year old man shouts.

"You need to hear what I think we need to do for Linda, Nelson," the patient physician is instructing.

"Tell it to Jewell and Nancy. Not me. I don't understand anything you say. What kind of doctor are you? Not a good one, that's for sure!"

The doctor's small black beeper box strapped onto his belt is ringing, but he isn't responding.

Nelson is wheeling himself to Linda's bed.

The youthful looking doctor walks out of the room and into the hallway, nearly bumping into a nurse in a blue smock who is speaking off-hand remarks into a cell phone while carrying a stack of medical charts, quickly followed by another nurse in a yellow smock hastily pushing a high tech code cart.

Nancy pushes her mother's wheelchair, to follow the physician out of the room. "I don't want my daughter to suffer, Doctor," Jewell is shouting loudly, trying to drown out Nelson's exclaiming "Why does Linda have to die?"

A blonde haired woman in a green uniform holding a bowl filled with red squiggling Jello is standing at the doorway. "Are you doing okay, Nelson?"

"Noooooooooooooo! I'm not doing okay. What do you think? Linda's dying! Don't you know that already?"

"Do you want a bowl of Jello?"

3

"It's about time you brought me something to eat!"

"I put your tray in your room, but I brought the Jello in case you don't want to go back to your room. Do you need me to help push you to your room?"

Nelson is crying as he is struggling to rise from his wheelchair. "I have to wee-wee. The stupid medicine from the stupid doctor isn't working. What's wrong with my bladder?"

The woman is trying to stop herself from crying.

"I'll take you back to your room, Nelson, or do you want to use Linda's bathroom?"

"Linda! I got to go wee-wee again and then I got to go back to my room and eat my lunch. I love you, Babe. Don't die while I'm gone."

Nelson's chest is heaving. "I think I'm having an asthma attack again," he shouts in panic.

The observing woman is turning her back to the scene, stepping into the hallway. "Everything is going to be okay, Nelson. Come on. I'll take you back to your room."

Nelson seats himself into his wheelchair, sniffling, coughing, and with the palm of his right hand wiping away the dripping mucus from his nose. Wheeling himself out of the room, he is shouting into the hallway, "Easy for you to say everything is going to be okay. You're wife isn't dying."

"I don't have a wife, Nelson. I have a husband."

"Too bad for you! And how come he don't come to see Linda? Didn't you tell him she's dying? I sent him a birthday card in April."

"You never forget anyone's birthday, do you, Nelson?"

For a few brief moments, Linda is alone in the room. But she is not forgotten amongst the hospital's staff. Every few minutes, a nurse, lab technician, a respiratory therapist, a janitor with a cleaning cart, is standing at the doorway looking in on her. Not out of responsibility; the monitors at the nursing station are performing that specific virtue; but in the name of love, compassion, and caring for a patient many have known for years. The staff of Westmoreland Hospital on each floor and in each unit from cardiology to the cafeteria know Linda and Nelson as chronic patients with bouts of chronic indigestion, asthma, obesity, and weak bladder, and the smallest aches and pains brought on by the couple's worst affliction, i.e., boredom.

In the sterile silence highlighted by the irritating but necessary life-sustaining buzzing and beeping of mechanical machines, fifty-four year old Linda is nearly dead to the world. But even in a coma she is sleeping with one eye open, a habit of hers since she was seven years old when she claimed to see a ghost at the doorway of her bedroom inside the impoverished white wooden house on the outskirts of her father's junkyard of broken down cars, refrigerators, stoves, ruined sofas and chairs, and rusty bathtubs.

At 12:20 p.m. inside Linda's hospital room in the historic town built and maintained by European immigrants and their descendants, thirty odd miles from Pittsburgh, there is no human being teasing and ridiculing her for being mentally retarded; a pattern of behavior she endured from others throughout her childhood and adolescence. There is no husband, mother, or siblings protecting her from cruel taunts and teasing from ignorant adults, and there are no professional health care providers advising her on progressive treatments. Most of all, there are no machines of modern science curing her. Yet, she is not alone, nor is she helpless.

With our eyes, we are unable to see the oblong beams of sparkling colored lights that are flowing out of Linda's body and ricocheting off the hospital room's ceiling, walls, floor, bed, lamp, sheets, pillows, flowers, chairs, blankets, and flowing back into Linda's chest. The penetrating lights are causing Linda's heart to relax, and the rays flowing upwards from her chest are quieting her mind, while the filters of transcendent rainbow hues are softening her lungs. Swirling atoms from a shining orange and yellow ball spinning above her forehead is illuminating her face, and the energized skin of her body is separating into tiny pink particles, with piece by piece being re-formed into translucent crystallized entities representing her physical appendages and limbs. Her whitish-turquoise hued spirit is now standing on the right side of the bed; with intense fascination she is looking down at her immobile body. She is slowly becoming aware that she is both witnessing and participating in the simultaneous separating and re-connecting of her mind, body, heart, and soul. But she is also feeling energized by the flow of the most delicate crystals twirling around her spiritual face.

She is hearing a soft voice whispering, "You feel as if you are being refreshed by the most delightful sunlight, don't you, Linda?"

Without moving her lips, Linda is hearing her own voice, "Where's Nelson?"

A perfectly beautiful man, standing in the midst of flickering flames of white fire, with a wide smile and cheeks moistened by glittering tears, is standing at Linda's side. "I am the Angel of Delight."

"I want Nelson. I can hear him crying."

"He went to his hospital room. The doctors are keeping him in the hospital so he doesn't have to be alone in the apartment. He will be back to say 'goodbye' to you when the assigned time is approaching, but for now I have come to give sustenance to your spirit so as to prepare you for your return journey into the Womb of Pre-Existence."

Linda's ghostly face is staring at her body lying in the hospital bed. "I want to see my Babe. He's sad because I'm so sick. I don't want to die. Nelson needs me."

"Your love for Nelson is the light which never stops sparkling. The Angels of Delight call it Primary Love."

"I have to take care of him because he takes me of me."

"Nelson exists for you and you for Nelson. That is why all things which you share together are delightful to one another. Joy shines within each of you. The gentle breathing of your spirits carries the flow of happiness onto the spirits of others who come into your presence."

"I don't understand what you're saying. I'm mentally retarded."

Out of the orange spinning disc, a flock of white birds with peacock colored feather tails are flying and circling Linda's dormant body. Linda is hearing the immaculate creatures singing in a most harmonious song. With intense power and immense grace, their feathers gently transform into white snowflakes, softly falling onto Linda's immobile body.

The Angel of Delight gently touches Linda's long brown hair now being covered by the flakes of crystal snow.

"You don't remember me, Linda, but I came to speak to you many times in your dreams before you got sick. The souls of angels do not have useless external thoughts, only profound internal images which bring delight to other angels, and often we transpose those beautiful images into your heart when you are asleep. That's how your mind knew that soon your soul and spirit would crystallize together, because you live in the pleasure of love, even when your brain is sleeping each earthly night."

"I don't understand what you are saying. I'm mentally retarded."

"Remember when? Before your body got sick? Your older brother Joey called you on the telephone and you suddenly said to him, 'Jooooeeeeeyyyyy, I think it's time for me to kick the bucket.' You said that from your energetic heart and shining soul blended together. Your heart and soul remember that I have whispered delightful words many times to you, in your dreams."

"I sleep with one eye open in case a ghost comes. I saw a ghost when I was a little girl and I was afraid and that's what made me mentally retarded. My mother told everyone it was the measles when I was six months old that made me mentally retarded. But I know it was the ghost."

"Ah. That wasn't a ghost you saw at the top of the staircase in your old house, Linda. That was me, the Angel of Delight. Perhaps you always slept, all through the years, with one eye open because your heart and soul were only looking for me to come back to you."

The white birds are weaving together the whirling white flakes of snow and transforming them into long white threads of silk, wrapping them around Linda's physical body.

"Remember when you were a little girl and you went to Kennywood Amusement Park? The first time you went on a roller coast?"

"It was only fun one time. I only went on it one time. I didn't want to go on it again."

"The long slow climb to the top and then fast, fast, fast down the steep tracks when you could hardly breathe."

"I was glad when it came to a stop and I could get out."

"Some people love the sensation of riding a roller coaster so much that they choose to go on it again and again and again. But others, like you, only decide to go on it once. It's the same as exiting and re-entering the Womb of Pre-Existence."

"I didn't like the roller coaster, but when I got off the roller coaster I sat down on the bench with my brother Joey. He likes roller coasters, and we ate pink and blue cotton candy together. I love my brother Joey. When we were kids he was the only person who could understand me. People thought I talked another language like Japanese. Kids teased me. They called me retarded. But Joey was my older brother and he could understand me. He lives in Reno now. I've never been there. I'm afraid of airplanes."

"Would you like to see him right now?"

"I can't go to Reno. I'm afraid of airplanes. And I can't leave Nelson."

"There is always a relationship between heavenly and earthly things, places, situations, and times because there is always an existing relationship between bodies and souls. Those separate entities and energies have different but corresponding beams of colorful lights which are designed and strengthened by the sparkling but invisible energies of love and wisdom combined, like the colors of a beautiful rainbow are joined together."

"I'm mentally retarded. I don't understand what you said."

"Oh, Linda, you're not mentally retarded anymore. Perhaps you never were. Perhaps you only thought you were because so many people told you that was who you were. But you will soon learn, throughout all the endless and numberless communities in the microcosm that you didn't exist outside your own perception of yourself."

With strands of pristine silk white threads wrapping around her sleeping face and slowly covering her mouth and nose, Linda's cracked mouth is inhaling and exhaling puffs of air which are escaping the beautiful coverings.

From the window pane, an eleven dimensional wheel is spinning towards her. The spinning orb is spraying glistening pink water, as resplendent as the color of ripe grapefruit, and green water, the color of morning dew forest grass, and red water as scintillating as burning fiery flames, and gold, tangerine, silver, lemon, copper, and cranberry sprays of water, resembling an explosion of liquid fireworks.

The Angel of Delight's smile is blazing with brightness.

"The spinning wheel is the components of your heart and soul combined, Linda, and the water is the fluid of love. Don't be afraid. It's beautiful Linda, because you are so beautiful."

While Linda's spirit is conversing with the Angel of Delight, throughout Greensburg people in family living rooms, cluttered business offices, noisy ethnic and fast food restaurants, sweet smelling donut shops, and in the smoke – filled bingo parlor, are telling stories about Linda.

A woman with green misty eyes, the director of a Greensburg vocational rehab center for developmentally disabled adults, with a smile on her face, is standing in line at a make-up counter of a department store, telling her teenage daughter, "Thirty-three years ago I had to fire Linda. She was never at her desk stuffing envelopes. Instead, she was always in the closet kissing Nelson."

In the teachers' lounge of the local high school, classroom, the music instructor is plucking the strings of his guitar and telling the hungry Vice-Principal, chomping on his wife's home-made spinach salad coated with white dressing, "I'd be in the grocery store with my family and all of a sudden from across the store I'd hear Nelson – as loud as could be – shouting our names. Right beside him would be Linda, laughing and eating her donuts. Before I knew it, my wife and kids and I would be helping them with their shopping, loading up their bags into our car, and driving them home. We didn't mind. Everybody in town who knows Linda and Nelson love them. Nelson is so funny and Linda never stops laughing. We just couldn't help loving them. It's a shame you never met them."

Three African American women, one anxiously waiting for the announcer to shout "G 58" so she can return a shout of "BINGO!" sit and struggle to find the words that can explain the sort of bewilderment each feels, the kind that plagues people when dealing with issues of life and death as if they are on a border of conscious rationality and emotional overflow.

"I sure do miss them not being here at afternoon bingo."

"What's going to happen to Nelson when Linda's here no more is more than I can bear to think 'bout. Darn! Why'd that man call G-57 instead of G-58?"

"That's 'cause you got bad luck today."

"All the times after Saturday night bingo I drove Linda and Nelson home to their little apartment so they didn't have to ride the bus at night or walk the dark streets? I sure do miss them not being here at bingo for so long"

"Linda is genuine. Most genuine person I ever met. Genuine girl. That's the word for that girl. Genuine. Come on, call my number, you blasted old man!"

Throughout Greensburg, for many people mourning the approaching death of Linda and the loneliness of Nelson, the combination of time, space, and matter is now a strangely surreal holograph.

And, in the Westmoreland Hospital on the third floor, nurses at the station and those walking up and down the corridor, are offering people courteous quick smiles, light embraces, trembling handshakes, and heartfelt words of comfort or condolence.

In Jewell's hospital room, she is barely listening to the discourse being offered by the physician because she is taxing her imagination by trying to picture the impending death of her daughter whom she has loved and taken care of for 22,541 days. Nancy is listening to the medical lecture, but interrupts her concentration, as does the physician, to listen to Jewell, who is spontaneously verbalizing her thoughts.

"Linda was always laughing. Remember when Linda got stuck in a restaurant booth? She was sooooo fat she couldn't get out of the booth and the waitress had to call the manager and he called men who came and took the table apart for Linda to get out of the booth. Linda was laughing so hard the whole time. The entire restaurant was laughing with her. She couldn't stop laughing. She was always laughing."

Nancy is mired in absolute grief at the suffering of her sister whom she shared a financially impoverished, emotionally turbulent, but culturally and spiritually enriched childhood with, and isn't feeling like releasing her tension with a chuckle or laugh.

While 3,651 miles away from Westmoreland Hospital, Linda's older brother Joey is delivering a speech to an audience of freshman college students.

"My life experiences, both exuberantly joyful and turbulently painful, have taught me that intense love manifests mystical and magical energy forces. I know that science has proven that energy cannot wither away, evaporate, and die. I believe that human energy is created, sustained, and perpetuated through the inherited physical, emotional, mental, and spiritual energies of ancestral roots. Energy is eternal and I can't help but wonder if spiritual energy is the color of pink?"

Students are exchanging facial expressions demonstrating confusion and amusement.

He is continuing his discourse, "As an avid genealogist, I am aware that my ancestors from Gaul and Phrygia adhered to the ancient concept of FATUM- believing that each person has a divinely assigned destiny. Do you know what your assigned destiny is? Perhaps something as great as discovering a cure for cancer? Perhaps something profoundly simple such as making people laugh. The question I pose to you for your contemplation is, 'can laughing one's way through life be someone's assigned destiny?'"

Joey can feel the vibrating of his cell phone in his left pants pocket.

"I want each of you to think about this particular statement from the Greek philosopher Lucretius, written many decades prior to the birth of Judaism and Christianity, 'Throughout the universe the various worlds are formed on various planes….the eternal whirling motions of the atoms bring together all which are like others in form. I want you to think about that ancient statement because it might help you to discover the secret to your fulfillment as a human being and as future professionals in the disciplines of child welfare, marriage and family therapy, nursing, and bereavement counseling, which the students in this elective class are preparing for, to my understanding. Or is there anyone here today studying to be a cosmetologist, auto mechanic, or flight attendant?"

The hidden miniature cell phone is vibrating.

"Is preparing for a professional career in the work of your choice merely your wish, dream, hope, interest, or is it your Fatum, your assigned destiny? For those of you who are married, engaged, have a boyfriend or girlfriend, ask yourself if your loved one is an element of your assigned destiny or only a mental and/or physical playmate based on your hormones and/or psychological needs. And finally, ask yourself, 'is my destiny shaped by the whirling of atoms?"

Rather than looking at the perplexed faces of his students, the 55 year old is retrieving his cell phone from his pants. Glancing at the illuminated contraption with black numbers against the green background, his feels his stomach start to tense up as he sees the area code signaling the caller isn't around the corner.

The sudden speed and strength of his heart's beating compels him to spray out the final words of his speech with quick heaviness.

"I don't think I'm wrong in assuming that each of your minds and, hopefully, your hearts are filled with bewildering questions and turbulent emotions from the little bits and pieces of what you have heard in the past 45 minutes. If many of you will be beginning your internships and hands-on experience for gaining permanent employment in working with people who are grieving, you need to constantly be questioning how you react to people's beliefs and feelings about what makes, as a famous song goes, 'the world goes round and round and round and round.' For instance, to make it a little personal so you grasp that I am speaking from both my heart and mind, I left home when I was 16 years old to roam the world in search for answers to questions. My sister Linda, who is one and a half years younger than me and diagnosed as either "emotionally disturbed," or "mentally retarded," stayed at home and replaced questions with laughter. I'm highly educated and she's practically illiterate, yet, I don't think she's ever had a sleepless night worried about her destiny, whereas I've never stop pondering mine, especially at 1:30, 2:30, 3:30 in the morning when I'm lying in bed and my eyes are peering through the darkness as I am staring at the ceiling and looking for something I think I should know. My questions demand answers whereas her laughter eradicates questions. What determines that I should be an inquisitive student of life and she a content genius of laughter? Genes? Luck? Astrological signs? Karma? Sins? For me, I believe it is my Fatum. Thank you. Think deeply."

With the clapping of hands together, the shuffling of papers and books, scuffing of shoes, and the low-keyed mumbling of confused, enlightened, entertained, and relieved students, bouncing off the oblong walls and high ceiling, the sixth blast of the Pennsylvania telephone number is blinking and vibrating furiously.

HIGHER THAN THE HEAVENS

"He who has the courage to laugh is almost as much master of the world as he who is ready to die. In this place everything I see or hear starts up an image of sweet remembrance. If you analyze well your most poetic impressions and imaginings of the ones that most exalt you and pull you outside of yourself and of the real world, the pleasure they cause consist totally or chiefly in remembrance."
Giacomo Leopardi

What we cannot see in Linda's hospital room are the trillions of bright red whirling atoms, each the color of brilliant blood, colliding with one another and exploding into swirling yellow clusters of blinking stars.

"Love is the fire of life," the Angel of Delight is telling Linda. Arching over the hospital bed is a golden bridge laden with shining red rubies, glistening white diamonds, and glowing green emeralds. The luminous angel whispers into Linda's ear, "It is the Bridge of Pneuma, the invisible energy connecting a person to their assigned destiny. Pneuma is an interior energy, an essence of joy which cannot die."

Linda's spirit is watching a procession of translucent men, women, and children walking in a graceful procession across the bridge. The visitors are emerging from the left wall, crossing the room, and exiting through the sun-heated window.

"I don't want to die, but I think I have to," Linda is crying.

"When you cross the Bridge of Pneuma and flow into the microcosm of Innumerable Affections, you retain all the delights of love you experienced in your heart when it was beating in your body."

"I don't understand what you said. I don't know if I'm mentally retarded or not anymore."

"You will never forget Nelson and he will never forget you. Love cannot die because love is energy and energy cannot disappear. It can only be misplaced or misdirected if the delight of love is ignored," the Angel of Delight informed her. "And when it is time, Nelson will cross the Bridge of Pneuma and be with you."

"If I go on that bridge with all those people, then I'm not going to see Nelson any more, am I?"

"Not with the brown eyes in your lovely face, but always in the crystal eyes within your soul."

"He's not going to cook my breakfast or lunch or dinner for me like he always does, is he? And, he won't be buying me any more donuts, will he?"

Linda is seeing large crystalline globes, flaming with silver and gold fire, spontaneously appearing in the ghostly white hands of the people walking across the bridge.

The Angel of Delight is stroking Linda's wet cheeks on her spiritual face as Linda is whispering, "I think my tears smell like rain."

"Those people, Linda, are entering the realm of Innumerable Affections. Inside those globes are their favorite memories of events which shaped and defined their lives."

"I don't have one of those balls."

"You haven't stepped onto the Bridge of Pneuma yet, Linda."

The Angel of Delight is pointing a long delicate finger into the blazing galaxy of violet and purple clouds and spontaneously sculpting pillars of chrysanthemum streams covering Linda's dying body in the hospital bed.

"I am taking care of the affections in your heart, Linda, and each cloud, pillar, and stream is an assigned affection which has its own energy which creates a memory of a place, a person, and an event."

Linda's spiritual right eye is releasing streams of yellow gaseous filaments flowing and fusing into various masses of colored energy particles, pushing the violet, purple, and chrysanthemum vapors aside.

Standing within the sweeping rainbow colored canvas is a smiling angel in the form of a pounding golden heart.

"I am your 'I', Linda. I am called the Angel of Beauty."

"Is Nelson coming back to see me?"

"Put your hand into my heart, Linda."

"I can't move my real hand."

"What is your own remains your own."

The snow white birds, twirling luminous white silk threads, are, one by one, transforming into round, square, rectangle, and oblong sheets of glossy three dimensional white papers with pink lettering.

"These papers are the information you have in your brain, Linda. Reach out and touch one."

To her astonishment, Linda's radiant pink spiritual fingers are feeling as if they are filled with bubbles. Stretching her glowing hand into the firmament, she is catching a fluttering document. Exploding into a magnetic field of crystals, the twirling atoms are fusing into a silver and glass metallic globe.

"Look inside the ball. What do you see, Linda?"

"There is too much light. I don't see anything."

"What do you feel?"

"I feel… I feel… I feel like I'm bouncing up and down like… like my body bounces when I'm riding the bus and it goes over bumpy roads and…it feels like I'm going somewhere… like I'm moving and not standing still… and I feel happy and scared at the same time and… I feel like I know a secret but I don't know what the secret is and…I feel like crying and laughing at the same time… and I feel like I'm alone but someone is with me… and… and…"

Linda's spirit is simultaneously crying and laughing and watching the Angels of Delight and Beauty growing smaller and twisting and turning into bedazzling geometric shapes and becoming miniature marionettes resembling Linda and Nelson as they were on the first day they met one another.

"I can see me sitting on a bus!" Linda is exclaiming. "And I can see Nelson sitting at a desk stuffing envelopes. Inside the rehab center! He's licking envelopes and telling people the glue tastes ucky! He's so funny!"

Sounds of Linda's jubilant laughing and sentimental crying are echoing throughout the resplendent galaxy of stars, birds, papers, silk threads, clouds, and making the rubies, diamonds, and emeralds decorating the Bridge of Pneuma, dance.

She is watching replicas of her and Nelson, as they once were, kissing one another, inside the sparkling globe.

Suddenly orange, red, and yellow tree leaves are floating in the round ball of light, each leaf forming a letter and number.

Autumn.1975.

Linda is seeing herself as a twenty-two year old blonde who is giggling. She is wearing a yellow gown with a white bow in her hair.

More leaves turning into letters and numbers appearing on a scroll.

Linda is hearing a melodious voice reading the words as they appear on a light brown scroll with orange script.

This day begins an 11,784 day love story between a developmentally disabled man and a mentally retarded woman. His red hair and moustache growing a shade brighter and her smile growing bigger, he yells, "*We're getting married!*"

"We got married on October 17. Thirty-three years ago!" Linda is exclaiming to the people walking across the Bridge of Pneuma.

The scene within the globe is evaporating and more autumn color leaves are swirling about, forming large gold letters.

God divided the light into darkness on the day they began their love story.

Linda is hearing a titanic voice telling her, "You and Nelson are made of atoms, Linda. And atoms can never die.. Never die.. Never die.. Never die. In the swirling dance of the colorful atoms, you will never die. And neither will the love you two have for one another.

Without seeing any of the spiritual world's elements, Nelson is entering the room. He is shouting, "Wake up, Babe!"

An ever-attentive social worker is following him into the hospital room. Extraordinary confusion is jointly engulfing both men as they are holding vigil for one man's wife and the other gentleman's client.

"You aren't killing her if you sign the papers to remove Linda from life-support, Nelson."

"Yes, I am! The doctor said that if he takes Linda off the machines she'll die in a few minutes!"

Nancy is entering the room. Her thoughts and feelings simultaneously and silently remind her that it has always been emotion and not reason that govern the decisions of her vulnerable family members. She is pushing Jewell's wheelchair. Linda's mother is fidgety, her wrinkled and crooked fingers nervously punctuating the air as she speaks.

"They should let me sign those papers. I'm Linda's mother. I've taken care of her for 54 years. I make all the decisions for Linda and Nelson."

"Mom, that's Pennsylvania law. Nelson has to sign the papers to remove the life-support equipment."

Nelson is loudly protesting, "If I sign the papers and they pull the tubes out of her arms and turn off the machines and she dies, the police will come arrest me for killing her!"

The social worker is perspiring lightly in the muggy room. "No, Nelson. The police won't arrest you. You aren't killing, Linda. She'll stop breathing in a matter of seconds. Her sufferings will be over."

The troubled husband, not willing to be an accomplice to the dictates of any person, is unable to replace his feelings of terror with any rational words of instruction. Nelson is releasing his anguish and fears in torrents of crying, coughing, and shouting.

"Why can't I sign the papers? I'm her mother. I've been taking care of her since she was born," Jewell is pleading in an angry voice.

"It's the law, Mom. You can't ignore the law. Nelson is Linda's spouse. He has guardianship."

With her wheelchair next her son-in-law's, Jewell is forcefully tapping Nelson's left hand. "Linda is suffering, Nelson. Sign the papers."

"You kill her, Jewell, and you go to jail! I'll come visit you! I'll bring you your Pepsi and cigarettes! I have to wee-wee again!"

Nelson, wheeling himself out of the room and into the hallway, is loudly threatening, "I'm going to sue everybody and then Linda and me will be rich and we'll get new doctors who know what they're doing!"

The social worker's face is showing signs of wear and tear caused from lightheadedness, claustrophobia and being over-heated. The sister's eyes conveying heartsickness, and the mother's voice broadcasting expansive outrage, are all emitting energies which do not affect Linda's death-like silence. But witnessing the energetic actions is Linda's crying spirit waiting for release and two compassionate angels, whose lights have been engulfing Linda's body and spirit.

"What am I going to do without her?" Jewell is muttering, crying softly.

"Linda is going to heaven, aren't you, Linda?" Nancy is smoothing her sister's hair.

The social worker is clearing his throat, sounding as if his air passage ways are filled with mucous. "I'll talk to Nelson again as soon as he is finished in the bathroom."

Jewell is stretching out her left arm. "Nancy, take my blood pressure."

"You're blood pressure is fine, Mom. I just took it a half an hour ago."

"I feel so tired. I need to die. Why should Linda die instead of me? I'm old. She's still young. 54 years old isn't old. I'm 77 years old. I'm old. It should be me dying and not Linda."

"We're all feeling tired, Mom."

"Did you call Joey in Reno?"

"Yes. He's coming here as soon as his daughter Anissa's wedding is over. She's getting married on the 18th. It's a Friday night. He told me he expects that the wedding will be over around 1:30 in the morning. He's going to go home, take a shower, pack his suitcase and he's catching the plane at 5:00 Saturday morning."

"Did you call Tommy and David?'

"Yes. David has to get his driver's license renewed so he can get on the plane, but he's coming in as soon as we call him and tell him that Linda is gone. And Tommy is starting his new nursing job, but he's going to come if he can, even if only for one day."

"My sons live in Reno, San Diego, and Las Vegas," she says to the social worker.

The social worker nods his head and offers Jewell a slight smile. "I know. Linda talked about them all the time."

"You're a good social worker. You've been very good to Linda and Nelson all these years."

"Thank you. Like everyone else in this town who knows them, and that's about half the town to say the least, I love them."

Nelson is re-entering the room. His facial expression is indicating his emotional indignation.

"And, I ain't signing those papers that's gonna make Linda die!"

During the last five words of Nelson's exclamation, the attending physician, a stethoscope hanging out of his white robe pocket, and a medical chart in his right hand, is walking into the room with quick steps.

"How are we doing?"

Nelson is spitting out his words, "Does it look like we're playing bingo? How come the medicine you gave me isn't helping my bladder?"

As the doctor is parting his lips to speak, Jewell is interrupting the on-going consultation. "Doctor, I think my lungs are congested. I feel like I can't breathe, even with my oxygen machine."

Nancy is rolling her eyes and biting down on her lower lip as her thin fingers continue to twist and straighten the long brown strands of Linda's hair. Nancy is saying aloud, "Her long hair was her pride and joy. She wouldn't let anyone tell her to get her hair cut. You loved your beautiful hair, didn't you, Linda?"

Having learned a long time ago the energetic behaviors of Nelson and Jewell, both frequent guests in the hospital, the physician is casually flipping the white and blue pages of the black metal, lime-green cover medical chart. He is letting the desperate mother and her son-in-law's comments pass without commenting.

The sizzling rays of the sun are glaring against the window pane.

Nurses, orderlies, and housekeeping staff walk past the room.

With a clutter of words in his mind, the physician is trying to formulate sentences with sensitive but firm words about Linda's condition. He is not willing to withhold the truth; but is momentarily silent in order to quell further outbursts of protest from Nelson and Jewell.

"It's so difficult when we have to let go of hope, but there is no hope for Linda to recover. It's not fair to any of you, and especially not fair to Linda, to prolong her death drama."

"Are you certain she won't wake up, doctor?"

"Linda's not going to wake up, Jewell."

With an intense ferocity, Nelson is shouting "Why not?"

Before the physician can turn his face to look at Nelson, the social worker is speaking. "Nelson, you need to sign the papers and let Linda go to heaven where she already is, really. She's not here. Only her body is here being kept alive by the tubes and machines. You know that."

"The only thing I know is that everybody is stupid! Except Nancy. Nancy isn't stupid."

"Thank you, Nelson, but you're not stupid either, Nelson. And neither is the doctor or social worker."

"I'm not stupid, either!" Jewell is proclaiming in self-defense.

"I want to go back to my room and think. I'm hungry. What time is dinner in this hospital or did all the cooks go on strike?"

Nelson, looking at his comatose wife, bolts his wheelchair and himself from the room.

"Don't die while I'm eating my supper, Babe! I'll be back! Wait for me !" he is proclaiming.

The weary and exasperated professionals in the room are silent, each wondering how to convince the stubborn husband to attach his signature to the legal documents. Neither is paying attention to Jewell while she is complaining "why is this happening to Linda? What did she ever do to deserve this kind of suffering? What did I ever do that was so bad to have to lose a daughter? I'm going to have a heart attack before this is all over."

Nancy, in rapt attention at the softness of Linda's skin, is wondering what thoughts are going through Linda's head as she is making her sacred transition from Greensburg, Pennsylvania to heaven.

Linda's physical frumpy arms are untainted and not scarred from needle marks. Overlying sheets are covering her swollen legs. Her puffy face is catatonic. Her breathing is slightly labored.

Jewell's voice is trailing off with the words, "Why does my Linda have to die? It's not fair. I'm so tired of burying everyone. First my sister Betty, then my father, then my husband, then all my sisters, and then my mother, and now my daughter. I'm so tired. I need to go back to my room. I'm the one who should be signing those papers. I'm her mother. I've been making the decisions about her life since the day she was born. I make all the decisions for Nelson, too. Nancy, when we get back to my room, I need you to take my blood pressure. I don't want to bother any of the nurses again."

Nervously reacting to her mother, Nancy is crying. The physician and social worker flee from the cramped room and step into the narrow hallway, the doctor nearly bumping into a laundry cart parked outside the room.

Linda's body is left alone again, lying beneath the fluorescent ceiling lights. But her weeping spirit is seeing the ghostly figure of a tiny old lady wrapped in many layers of colorful skirts, a long white blouse, and a red, blue, green, and yellow flower scarf covering her head, wisps of yellowish white hair sticking out of the silk head garb.

Linda's spirit is standing paralyzed in a gusty snow storm. The wind beating against her face is so cold that she is telling her dormant body, "I hope my blood doesn't turn into red ice."

At the foot of Linda's hospital bed, the old woman is stretching out both of her hands, collecting falling snow flakes; but, as each flake touches her bare hands, it changes into a purple plum. Within seconds, she is offering Linda's shivering spirit a glistening cluster of frozen violet fruit balls. Linda opens her mouth to speak, but the whipping wind immediately burns her throat. The little old lady struggles to walk through the storm, the wind knocking her around and the snow blinding her eyes. She is carefully grasping the cold steel frames, covered with icicles, of Linda's hospital bed.

"I don't want to be here alone," Linda cries, her spiritual fingers gripping those of her physical body's hands.

"Your ancestors are waiting for you in the plum tree field known as the Field of Good Fortune. Surrounded by the endless number of plum trees is a golden meteorite, Linda. It came from the battle between the Dorba Kob-the Energy of Good Fortune- and the Zla Kob-the Energy of Evil Fortune. Your ancestors believe that if you touch the meteorite while your pre-existent soul is in the Field of Good Fortune, that when you are born on earth, you will be assigned your destiny, and it will be one of beauty, meaning, joy, and all your wishes, dreams, and hopes will come true."

"I don't know what you are talking about," Linda's spirit is whispering, covering her body's mouth with her shivering hands. "I'm so cold."

"You are cold because your body is preparing itself to release your soul. During the dying process, first the mind separates from the body, then the spirit, and finally the soul."

Linda's spirit is feeling that her physical eyes are burning from the pounding freezing wind. Peering through the gusts of snow, Linda's spiritual eyes are seeing gigantic swaying trees with large shining purple plums dangling from the long snow covered branches above her hospital bed.

"When children become adults on earth, many don't know if they should keep or throw away the clusters of plums from the Field of Good Fortune," the lady proclaims in a melodious sing-song voice.

Linda's spirit is looking at a group of women, wrinkles in their chubby sunken faces, their semi-oriental eyes glaring back at her. Each is wearing a multi-colored outfit of skirt, blouse, and head scarf. Each is standing around the hospital bed.

"Hello, Linda. I am Veronica Bagaria Galata, your great-grandmother from Turkey."

"I am Susan Dobrancian Petrick Andrejchak, your great-grandmother from Slovakia."

"I am Margaret Stone, your great grandmother from Nova Scotia."

"I am Mary Pirero, your great-great grandmother from Portugal."

"I am Margaret Slaney, your great grandmother from Toppensham."

The elderly ladies are forming a walking caravan, strolling down a snow covered stone path which is circling the hospital bed. As they are walking, Linda's spirit is following, and noticing that the snow is falling faster, the wind growing colder, and her nervousness becoming stronger. She is feeling as if her body's fingers are craving for a fire's flames.

"We are here to help you fulfill one last act of your Fatum, your assigned destiny," the ladies are singing in soprano and alto voices- in unison- as if they are members of an all-women choir.

"My body is freezing to death."

"Death is a very piercing storm, we're afraid," one of the ladies is telling her, with an apologetic tone to her accented voice.

Linda's spiritual eyes are trying to get a better look at the crooked fingers of all the ladies as each is gently collecting falling snow flakes and watching them turn into purple plums. Snow is now covering Linda's physical pink fingers and her spirit is feeling like blowing on them to thaw them out. Linda's body is twitching as she is wrapping her spiritual arms around her body's chest. Again, she is carefully walking through the snow storm towards the golden boulder in the center of the circle, sitting on top of Linda's stomach. Each woman has an ecstatic expression on her old-fashioned face.

"I can't turn around and go back inside you," Linda's spirit is telling her physical face.

Linda's spiritual eyes are seeing a group of elderly men, many wearing old uniforms once worn by steel-mill workers and one man wearing a very old sailor's uniform and cap, appearing and walking in a procession towards the golden meteorite.

"Hello, Linda. I am your great-great-great-great –great-great-great grandfather. I am Jonas Stone. A fisherman from England who settled in Newfoundland."

Suddenly Linda's purple lips on her physical face are moving, trying to form words, while her body's legs are twitching and her stomach is rumbling. She is pointing a spiritual index finger at the men. "I don't know you or you or you or you or you or you, but I remember you. You are Grandpap Galata!"

A gregarious smile on his large face beneath his bald scalp, the man Linda's spirit is recognizing is stepping towards her. Linda's spiritual arms are reaching out to him, but without warning all the men and women, one by one, begin to disappear.

"I don't want to be alone!"

Linda's spirit is trying to run through the snow storm to the vanishing figures, but she isn't able to move her feet and legs which are buried in purple snow.

Wearing a long white nightgown matching her white hair, an elderly woman with a beautiful smile, her face being illumined with crystal blue rays, her arms outstretched in the snow blowing wind, is leaning against a plum tree. She is holding a burning candle, the bright orange, red, green, yellow, and blue flame dripping wax onto the snow. She is radiant.

"My Linda!"

Looking at her, Linda is laughing and exclaiming, "Grandma Slaney!"

"I'm here for you, Linda."

"I want to go back inside my body, Grandma. I have to say 'goodbye' to Nelson and to my mommy."

"Everyone is getting ready to say 'goodbye' to you."

Linda's maternal grandmother is pulling Linda's spirit into her arms and placing her trembling head into her long cupped fingers.

"Linda. I must tell you, that soon Nelson is going to be signing the papers to remove you from the machines that are keeping you on earth. He is scared that the police are going to come get him because he thinks that by signing the papers he is killing you."

"I don't want my Nelson to be scared or sad, Grandma."

"No. That is why I am going to help you give him one last gift which he will remember for the rest of his life without you."

"When Nelson signs the paper and the doctor takes away the machines, will I be dead?"

"You will then come back to the Kingdom of the Living with me. It is so beautiful there, Linda. I've been here for a long time now and I'm so happy. You never met my daughter Betty, Linda, because she died when she was a teenager many, many, many years before you were born. All the while I was growing older and older, I always thought of my Betty. And when it was time for the Angel of Delight to come to see me while I was in the hospice, the Angel of Delight took me to see my Betty. And I am with my daughters Jane and Helen and Charlotte again. Someday, Linda, the Angel of Delight will bring Nelson to you."

"But I don't want Nelson to stay in Greensburg being scared that he killed me and being scared the police are going to put him jail. I know that isn't true. I don't know, Grandma, how I know that. But I know it's not true."

"Because you are feeling an over-whelming sensation we call the genuine truth. Remember when everyone in the family always used to say 'what's going to happen to Linda when she grows up?' And I would always tell them, 'don't you worry about Linda. She's genuine. Worry about yourselves.'"

"I need to make Nelson believe it is okay to sign the papers to take away the machines and to know that I died only because …. Because… Because…

"Because it was your assigned destiny and not because Nelson signed the papers."

"How can I tell him that?"

"You can't tell him. But you can show him. Easily."

"How?"

"Our ancestors believed that there are spinning spheres giving certain people, whose souls, hearts, and spirits are highly developed, extra-ordinary powers of love, wisdom, and truth. You and Nelson have always lived in those magical spheres."

A rip-roaring noise of voices jolts Linda's spirit's attention. Her physical eyes are opening and with her eyes uncontrollably darting side to side, her mouth hanging open, and her throat burning, Linda's spirit is searching for the source of the voices, but she is seeing no ancestors or angels except for Grandma Slaney's spirit.

"Linda, I want to tell you that death is not the end of life. A person does not have one form, but two, one form for appearance given to him or her by the parents, and an invisible form given by the dust of ancestors. When there is death, the first form is destroyed, but the dust of the second form returns to the Field of Good Fortune, to the place of FATUM," the sparkling spirit of her maternal grandmother is saying.

"My body's lips and nose are freezing to death, Grandma!"

Clouds of white fog are floating from behind a cluster of tall trees coming up from the hospital floor. Bending over her physical body, her spiritual fingers gliding down her physical face, Linda's spirit is feeling a burst of energy exploding in her body.

"It's alright, Linda. Everyone has an over whelming fear of dying."

Linda's spirit feels that she is sinking into freezing water, pain pricking every inch of her physical torso, limbs, and face. But she also feels that she is supercharged with more intense energy than she has ever felt.

"This is what it feels like in the last stages of life before the first moments of death," Grandma Slaney's spirit whispers.

Linda's spirit watches circles of frosty breath escaping her physical mouth and floating into the snowy thick air.

"I have to help Nelson, Grandma. I can't die until I give him the last gift."

Linda's spirit feels that the last atoms of bodily warmth are nearly gone. Looking up at her grandmother, Linda's spiritual silver tears are frozen onto her violet crimson cheeks.

A bright orange and yellow beam of sunshine is breaking through the snow storm. Numberless pink and purple plum tree blossoms float in the air, mixing with the snow flakes. Slowly, Linda's spirit is stretching her arms into the sunshine.

Walking in musical rhythm towards Linda's body and spirit, are the re-appearing female ancestors, carrying loaves of bread, jars of honey, and sweet cakes. Behind them are the male ancestors, carrying rusty iron shovels and buckets of fiery red steel nuggets, singing in Slovakian, Turkish, Portuguese, and English, their voices harmonizing. One- by -one the ancestors kiss Linda's frozen forehead.

VASTER THAN THE HEAVENS

"To heaven, to you, ye gentle souls, I swear no base desire intruded on my thought; but with a pure and sacred flame I burned. The flame still loves, and that affection pure, still in my thought that lovely image breathes, from which, save heaven, I no other joy have ever known; my only comfort now. Your love will ever follow me, and will yet cling to me when this body, which indeed no longer lives, shall be turned to ashes, forever. Love is the generator of all things beautiful. The first ecstatic moment of love, the joy of such beauty." Giacomo Leopardi

Everyone in Linda's room is looking world-weary. Jewell and Nancy, holding one another's hands, are standing on the right side of Linda, clasping her hand of non-moving fingers. A nurse, her glasses perched on the end of her pointed nose, with a glass-eyed gaze, is squeezing her fingers into latex gloves. In the far corner of the quiet room, the physician flipping through Linda's medical chart, and the social worker fidgeting with his I.D. badge, are quietly confirming to each other that Nelson is not going to change his mind.

Wearing a grey suit, white shirt, and long blue tie, Nelson wheels himself into the room. Everyone is taken back. For the first time in over a week, the soon-to-be widower has taken a shower, shaved, and dressed in clothes other than a hospital gown and pair of pajamas.

"What you all staring at? You never seen anyone in a suit before? I got to look handsome for my Linda when I say goodbye to her."

There are no personal or medical exchanges of pleasantries. In silence, Nancy is kissing Linda's forehead.

"I already said my goodbyes. Just turn off the life support machines and let Linda die in peace," orders Jewell.

Struggling to stand upright, Nelson is sobbing. "Bye, Babe! I'll see you soon, Babe! I love you, Babe!"

None of the three professionals in the room are sticking to the routine of obligatory health care protocol by practicing emotional detachment. Each allows tears to cloud their eyes.

"Married for thirty-three years, Linda and Nelson were heaven's gift to the other," the social worker whispers to the physician who nods in agreement.

Nelson slumps into his wheelchair and without issuing another word, wheels himself out the door. "Why does she have to die?" he is bellowing in the hallway.

Trying hard to be on her best professional behavior by swallowing her tears, the nurse is wearily watching the monitors as she disconnects tubes and technological circuitry.

Everyone is holding their breath waiting for Linda's death to commence.

"It will be a matter of minutes, Jewell," the physician whispers.

"I just want her to go in peace. I don't want her to have any pain."

"She's not going to feel any pain, Mom."

"54years ago I gave birth to her," Jewell is telling everyone, not knowing or caring if anyone is listening. "She was born on April 24. McKeesport Hospital. I picked the name Linda. My mother-in-law said it wasn't a Catholic name and the priest wouldn't baptize her without a Catholic name. So I picked Catherine for her middle name. She was baptized at St. Mary's. Her father's brother Don was her godfather. I forget who her godmother was. Nobody on my side of the family was Catholic. We were all Episcopalians. I had to convert so I could marry Linda's father Joe. Linda was born normal. But she got the measles when she was six months old. That's what made her retarded. Is she still breathing?"

The nurse is nodding her head.

"She's breathing on her own, Mom," Nancy says, patting Linda's hands and smoothing the skin on her forehead. "The machines are turned off now."

Jewell is looking at the physician. "You said it would only take a minute or two."

"It looks like she's struggling to hang on to the edge of her life," replies the physician.

"You never know, Mom, how long it can take once they remove the life support."

"I don't need to be here. I already said my goodbye. Nancy, take me back to my room. Someone can come tell me when Linda's gone. I can't take this anymore. I'm going to have a heart attack. Goodbye, Linda. I love you. I love you, Linda. I love you."

The physician is taking command of the room. "I think we ought to leave and let Linda die in peace."

Jewell turns her wheelchair around and leaves. In the hallway, she shouts, "I hope none of your nurses ever have to bury one of your children. It's not fair. Not fair at all for a mother to bury one of her children."

Nancy kisses Linda's forehead again and is smoothing strands of her long brown hair. "Bye, Linda. Joey, David, and Tommy are coming home. Me and Mommy will take care of Nelson for you. Be happy in heaven, Linda."

The nurse is whispering that Linda's breathing has stabilized without the life support technology.

The doctor is glancing at his wrist watch and the social worker is looking up at the wall clock. As the health care professionals are exiting the room, not one is pausing at the door and turning to look back at the woman whose life story was coming to an end. As fragile as she is, Linda is breathing on her own, despite the poor performance of her vital signs.

But Linda's comatose body is not alone.

Standing at the bedside is Linda's beautiful white spirit. Her self-identity of "I." She is glowing as if she were a resplendent fiery tail trailing a shooting star.

Inside the hospital room, Linda is split in two. Her spirit and body are disuniting.

"I, "Linda is whispering to her dormant body, "have to stay with you for a few more hours to give Nelson one last gift. Together we have to show him that by taking the body off life support, he did not kill me and that Greensburg police aren't going to come and arrest him."

Standing at the doorway is another angel. She is glowing like the flickering orange flame of a candle. From her eyes is a long white beam flowing onto Linda's body.

"I am the Angel of Absolute Beauty. I am at the death bed of each and every person who lives in the domain of beauty. I whisper the Energy and Wisdom of Beauty into the ears of the dying person. I am the Reflection of Beautiful Creative Love Who Knows Reality. I will stay here with your body and spirit, Linda, until the final separation occurs."

"How long will that be?"

"It is the Beautiful Spark of your love for Nelson which is delaying your assigned time to return to the Sea of Pre-Existence, Linda. The energies of your own innocence and love are so strong and resonant that the Angel of Repentance has no need to come with me to your separation moments. Your soul, Linda, has always been filled with the Gifts of Beauty. Your disabled mind, what people called 'mentally retarded,' was also a gift from your ancestors so as to hide the beauty of your heart from blinding others whose tarnished consciences could not understand the beautiful energies you possess. Remember when the nuns at your catechism class would tell you that your Jesus said to those who walked with him on this earth, 'Blessed are the pure in heart; for they shall see God.' Linda, you have been one of those pure in heart."

A nurse on her rounds, handing out medicines to the patients in the third floor rooms, is stopping at the doorway into Linda's chamber. Motionless, she is intently eyeing the comatose body. Her eyes are following every slow motion of Linda's breathing. "Gonna do it on your own time, ain't you, Linda? We're gonna miss you, Linda. We'll take care of Nelson for you. Don't you worry. You just go when you need to be going."

Linda's spirit is staring at her body. She is turning to the Angel of Absolute Beauty. "I wish I could see my brother Joey. He's so far away."

"Thoughts are energy, Linda, and energy never dies."

"He couldn't come to see me because he daughter is getting married in two days. I wish he was here with me when it's time for me to leave. Joey was there when my mommy and daddy brought me home from the hospital when I was born. Now that it's time for me to leave the hospital because I'm dying, I wish...."

"Would you like to tell him to hear the words in your heart?"

"How?"

"Look, Linda."

Stretching out her long orange fingers, the Angel of Absolute Beauty is pointing to the window. On the glass is the reflection of the spirit of a man who is twirling in circles, stomping his feet, twisting his body. It is an energetic mirage of his spirit being engulfed in white flames of fire.

"That's Joey. My brother. He's dancing in the fire! It's not a dream! He is crying and dancing. Joooooeeeeeeeyyyyy!" Linda's spirit is trying to cross the window towards the window. But she isn't able to move away from her body.

"Dear sweet Linda. Your eldest brother's body is many thousands of miles away from this room. But I wanted you to see that the energies of his heart are here in this room with you. When your sister Nancy held up her cell phone to your body's ears this morning, what did Joey whisper to you?"

"I heard his voice coming through the phone. But I can't remember what he said."

Linda's spirit stares at the dancing image on the window pane. "He is dancing so fast. Why is he dancing inside white fire?"

"At this moment, many, many miles away from Greensburg, his spirit and body are twirling, stomping, shaking, twisting together as he is dancing because he is being united with the Pneuma, the Spanda, the Duende, and his Fatum, and that is causing the white fire. The fire of love."

"I don't know what all those words mean."

Throughout the room, Linda is hearing her brother's words floating in the air. "I love you, Linda. You are the most beautiful sister in the world. I always knew you were an angel on this earth. Tonight I'm going to dance for you. I dance like our ancestors danced. Our great ancestors from Turkey and Slovakia and Toppensham and Gaul danced to worship God, honor their ancestors, tell God 'thank you,' supplicate our needs, and fulfill our destiny. I'm going to dance for you tonight that you will be with our ancestors in heaven because you have fulfilled your assigned destiny, Linda. You were put onto this earth to show people that angels really do exist. You are an angel, Linda. I love you. And I'm going to tell everyone what a beautiful angel you were on earth and in heaven. The Pneuma is the Energy of Life and your energy is so beautiful, Linda. The Spanda is the Energy of Vibration and your vibrations are so beautiful, Linda. The Duende is the Energy of Inspiration and you have always given people beautiful inspiration, Linda. The Fatum is the Energy of Destiny and your purpose in life was to teach people beauty of the heart, Linda. I love you, Linda. I am dancing for you."

"I love you, Jooooooeeeeyyyy."

"He loves you, Linda."

"When we were little kids, he was the only one who could understand me. People made fun of the way I talked. Nobody could understand me. Only my brother Joey."

From the Angel of Absolute Beauty, rays of various red and pink hues are flowing from her mouth as she is speaking.

"That's because your brother could always feel the beauty in the words that came from your heart, Linda."

"He is dancing like he was in the middle of a tornado."

"The vibrations of love."

"When we were children, we were in a tornado. On a Saturday night. The old church fell down onto of our house. We were hiding in the corner with a candle. I was scared. I was holding Joey's arms. I was crying. I could hear Joey praying to the Virgin Mary. Hail Mary, full of grace...."

"Pray for us now and at the hour of our death."

"I want to say 'goodbye' to my brother Joey."

"What do you want to tell him, Linda?"

"I want to tell him.... I want to tell him... I want to tell him..."

"Say it Linda. He will hear your spirit while he is dancing. It is a gift given to him by your ancestors. When he is dancing, he can hear the voices of those in the Kingdom of Heavenliness."

"Joooooeeeeyyyyyy. I'm not retarded anymore."

The contour of the dancing spirit is changing while twirling, twirling, twirling, in a circle. His bare feet are stomping harder and harder while he is spinning. His arms are opening wider and wider, higher into the air while he is twirling.

Spinning purple atoms are floating out of the window and throughout the room, hovering over Linda's spirit. Above her body, the violet atoms are transforming into hundreds of miniature glass mirrors, weaving a constellation of sparkling images. Inside each piece of shining glass is Linda's smiling face when she was a child.

"That's me in those mirrors!" Linda's spirit is exclaiming with glee.

"Your brother is thinking of your childhood together. He is seeing images of you in his memory bank. The faster he is dancing, the more images he is seeing."

"That's me when I was twelve years old. In my red majorette uniform and I was marching in the parade. I was twirling my baton. I was too old and too big to march with the little girls so I had to march all by myself. People laughed at me. They made fun of me."

"Your brother Joey was so proud of you when you were marching down the street in McKeesport."

"I wanted to be a majorette. I didn't care if they laughed at me or not. And look at me in that mirror! That's when I made my first Holy Communion! I remember that Sunday. I was seven years old. All dressed up in my white veil and white dress. I practiced my first confession with Joey who pretended he was the priest. We practiced on our front porch. He said "Tell me your sins." I said 'I don't got no sins.' He told me that I couldn't tell that to the priest in real confession. But I did. When I went to my first real confession at St. Mary's, I said to the real priest, "I ain't got no sins." Father Idzik said to me, "Everyone has sins." I said, "Maybe you, but not me."

Sparkling multi-colored glittered falls out of each miniature mirror and onto Linda's dormant body.

"The path is being cleared, Linda."

"I want to know if Joey heard what I told him."

"Tell him again, Linda."

"Joooooeeeeyyyyy. I'm not retarded anymore!"

A chorus of angelic voices is singing "Thou hast named her Linda… Thou hast named her Linda…." Rhythmic pounding of drums…. "Thou hast named her Linda…." Pious music of flutes… "Thou hast named her Linda…" Plucking of harp strings…. "Devoted to beauty… Thou hast named her Linda."

"Jooooooeeeeyyyyy. I'm not retarded anymore!"

Within the music, Linda hears her brother's powerful booming voice, "You never were, Linda! You never were!"

The phenomenon of the beautiful lady at the doorway is glowing so brightly the room is filled with white light. Linda's spirit is feeling herself floating towards the Angel of Absolute Beauty.

"Goodbye, Nelson. Goodbye, my Babe. We'll be together soon, Nelson. I love you, Babe!"

Linda's spirit is flowing through a spectacle of pink sword-like shafts, greenish-blue fluorescent lightning bolts, a rainbow spinning solar disk, wisps of white smoke, a reddish swirling of mass atoms, and zillions of dark green, light green, yellow-green, white-green blinking stars. She is being absorbed into a silvery cloud resembling a meadow of crystallizing snow illumined by countless rays of the yellow twirling sun. She is hearing a symphonic choir singing strange sounding words, "*Noli dolere, amica, eventum meum.*"

While soaring through whitish-red sunlight, Linda is looking for the human figures who are chanting above the singing, "We are the Angels of Fata…We are the Angels of Fata…." but she is only seeing a blue and white ocean of turquoise balls surrounded by golden beams.

"We appear as Landpools and Skypools because we reflect the bright destinies of those who once-upon- a- time left the Sea of Pre-Existence and walked upon the darkness of earth beneath the illuminated sky."

"Who is talking to me? Who is singing? Where am I?"

"We are the voices of the Angels of Fate. "*Noli dolere, amica, eventum meum.*" We sing for you, "*Do not sorrow, my friend, about my destiny.*"

"Where am I?"

A rainbow light is forming an arch of emerald water. A flying white dove is speaking, "You have returned to the Sea of Pre-Existence, Linda."

"Where is that?"

"It is inside your soul."

"It is where your passions come from."

"I feel like crying."

The dove is transforming into a spinning topaz stone while saying, "That is because your heart can feel the energies of the hearts of those who have love for you. Would you like to see and hear the energies of Nelson's anguish, your mother's sorrow, your sister's torment, your brothers' confusion, dejection, and broken heartedness, and the grief of your uncles, aunts, cousins, doctors, nurses, therapists, social workers, and your friends as they mourn together in Greensburg to say 'goodbye' to your body? Their hearts are united in private grief and public mourning. The strength of their turbulent energies combined is so powerful that you can perceive their thoughts and emotions which are sown in their hearts and reaped in their minds."

A phenomenon of razor hedged hail stones is exploding, the wind and hail growing faster and larger. Ice covered rocks are being swept up by a coarse howling wind. Linda feels frightened as the hail stones are pounding upon her.

"This storm, Linda, is the tears and grief of Mokosh, Wet-Mother Earth, as your Slavic ancestors called the Source of Life."

Through the torrent of hail stones, Linda is seeing a wide elongated sheet of glass framed by golden fire. Inside the mirror, is a large purple plum tree covered with sparkling icicles standing in an immaculate white field of snow.

She hears a man's voice saying, "I am the Angel of Eternal Memory. You are now a memory in many people's minds because your image remains in their hearts. There is no darkness in eternity because time remembers everything. Step into my reflection, Linda."

Linda floats into the glass. She is seeing the people she loves as they approach her body in the pink and white casket. In ancient Slavic tradition, the older women and men are gently kissing the cold face of Linda, offering her a last expression of love to prevent her spirit from roaming from house to house of relatives and friends in search for a last kiss.

"What's going to happen to Nelson without me now?"

Floating around Linda's body in the casket is a brilliant display of translucent bubbles which turn the earthly room into a sphere of silver rain drops.

The voice of the Angel of Eternal Memory says, "Don't be afraid, Linda, of the rain drops. Each drop is the imprint of the incorruptible ornament of love which you felt while you were on earth. The people who love you in the Patalone Funeral Home cannot see the bubbles or rain drops."

Linda laughs and speaks aloud, "One time when I was 12 years old, it was really raining hard. We were going to church. My dad and mom were sitting in the car waiting for me, Joey, David, Nancy, and Tommy to run outside and jump into the car. Tommy and David went first; and they didn't care if they got wet. Nancy had a little girl's red umbrella. But when Joey ran out into the rain he shouted at me, 'Linda, don't let the raindrops melt you!' I thought that was so funny that I stopped running and stood on the sidewalk in the rain and laughed so hard. I couldn't stop laughing. My mother had to get out of the car and take me back inside the house so I could put on a new dress."

"The bubbles are the ether of prayers people are saying for you, Linda."

Linda is looking at herself lying in her final sanctuary, her long brown hair draped over her shoulders with two silver clips placed by Nancy. In her hands are a pink and white rose with a card stating *Nelson.* Standing at the corner of the casket in between two bouquets of floral arrangements, keeping vigil over her best friend, is Diane, a deaf mute. Diane is composing her emotions before another attack of silent weeping.

Speaking softly, Linda's spirit begins to laugh. "Diane was my bridesmaid at my wedding. She taught me sign language. My wedding day was the most beautiful day of my life. I will never forget that day. Never forget. I wore a yellow gown. My Uncle Jim walked me down the aisle because my daddy was home lying in bed, he was dying of cancer. I was scared people were going to laugh at me like they did when I was a majorette in the parade. But nobody laughed. Everyone told me I was beautiful."

Linda's body inside the pink and white casket is being surrounded by metallic colored rings.

"Am I inside a rainbow?"

The silver water drops floating in the Patalone Funeral Home are interacting with the colored rings and forming balls of white foam.

"Am I inside a cloud?"

From the pink and white roses in Linda's hands, lightning bolts are flashing.

"Am I inside a rain storm?"

Snow starts falling onto Linda's body.

"Am I inside a snow storm?"

A yellow and orange light beam fills the entire spectrum.

"Am I inside the sun?"

Linda is looking at the grieving people in the room. She sees colorful cosmic dust swirling in the air. She hears the voice of the Angel of Eternal Memory saying, "You are inside the layers of beauty which come from the Supreme Beauty and which is Life Itself and removes all negativity, doubt, and cynicism from the soul which is manifested in the heart which is formed in the Sea of Pre-Existence."

"I can see Nelson and I can see my mother, but I can't touch them."

"They can't see you or hear you, Linda. But you can see and hear them."

Linda watches Nelson, wearing a light grey suit, white shirt, and blue tie, and rising from his wheelchair. His chest is heaving from labored breathing. A nurse is dislodging Nelson's hands from the steel arms of the wheelchair. He is loudly lamenting "Bye, Babe! I'll see you soon, Babe! Why did you have to die, Babe?!"

With a gentle voice, Linda's spirit is whispering into Nelson's ear, "Don't cry for me, Nelson. I'll be alright. I'll watch over you, Babe! I'll take care of you from here. You can't see me or hear me Nelson, but I'm alright. Don't cry, Nelson. Your asthma will start up."

Nelson's groaning and moaning is being followed by Jewell's "I love you, Linda!" recurring refrains, as she stands looking at Linda's face for the last time. Linda's spirit is whispering into her mother's ear, "I'm okay, Mommy. Take care of Nelson. I'm okay. I saw Grandma Slaney. She's going to take care of me. And I saw Grandma Galata and Grandpa Galata, they are going to take care of me, too. I haven't seen Daddy yet, I don't know where he is. But maybe I will see him and tell him that I was very, very happy being Nelson's wife."

Both Nelson and Jewell are now complaining about having trouble breathing, both being too tired to stand, and being too weak to handle any more stress.

The handsome young mortuary attendant, Jeff, ushers people into the adjoining room. The funeral parlor is now empty except for Linda and a group of stoic men dressed in black suits.

Linda's spirit is watching the strangers lowering the lid of her pink and white casket.

"I'll never see myself again and nobody will ever see me again."

The Angel of Eternal Memory embraces Linda's spirit. "But you are not gone, Linda, nor will you ever be forgotten. For love cannot die. Love never dies."

Mourners sit on wooden chairs, passively staring at a preaching minister, a signing social worker, and a guitar playing musician. Mourners are giving their undivided attention to Nelson who is sobbing. Mourners are thinking about the past funerals of their loved ones and trying to chase away intruding images of their own future funerals. None of the mourners question the where-about of Linda, each knows that she is no longer in the Panatalone Funeral Home with them, but inside a closed coffin lying in a shiny black hearse in the driveway.

The Angel of Eternal Memory's voice says to Linda's spirit, "You will now walk unhindered through the layers of beauty in the Kingdom of the Living where there is no time."

Linda's spirit is listening to the glorious harmony of choral voices singing, "For thine is the kingdom, and the power and the glory…."

"I'm scared to be all by myself in the grave. Before I married Nelson I was always with my mommy. Then for thirty-three years I was living with Nelson. I was never away from him. Every time he had to stay in the hospital, I stayed with him. Every time I had to stay in the hospital, he stayed with me. Now my body is alone in the casket. It's dark in there. I don't like the dark. My mommy should have told the men in black suits to open one of my eyes. I always slept with one eye open because I was afraid of the dark. It was always so silent in the dark. I was afraid of the silence."

"But now, Linda, your soul will be with the Angels of Philokalias.

"With who?"

"The Angels of Philokalias. The angels who radiate the highest Light and Sound of Beauty."

"I don't know who they are."

"When you were a little girl, Linda, what was your favorite thing to play?"

"None of the kids wanted to play with me because I was retarded. So I had to play by myself a lot. When nobody was looking at me, because I didn't want people to tease me, I would pretend I was a singer. I would pretend to sing beautiful songs and pretend everyone would be clapping for me."

"Now people in the Patalone Funeral Home are going to applaud you, Linda. Watch and listen."

Linda is seeing her Joey standing at the wooden podium. He is looking at the plethora of multi-racial and multi-ethnic people, gently touching one another's hands in individual humane reassurances that death is not the end of life.

"When Linda and I were growing up, we were only one-and-a-half years apart in age, I heard relatives, neighbors, teachers, and even strangers ask one another the same old question, *'What is going to happen to Linda when she grows up?'*"

Linda notices that Jewell is nodding her head.

"There are two answers to that long ago question. The first answer came thirty-three years ago."

Linda is seeing that Nelson's chest is heaving, his eyes are watering, and his voice is cracking with an inaudible sound.

"The other answer came inside this funeral home. When I came to this funeral parlor, I didn't know what to expect, and frankly, I had a few preconceived notions. What I found was that Linda and Nelson together had created a community. If you look around this room, you see bingo players, bakery clerks, social workers, therapists, nurses, bus drivers, taxi drivers, shopping mall clerks, bingo players, bingo players, and more bingo players. There are people here with academic titles sitting next to people with mental and physical disabilities, not as caregiver to client, but as peers. In a town that is still, in its own historical way, old fashioned, there are in this room together, descendants of Eastern European, African, Nordic, Asian, Middle Eastern, Western European, Latino immigrants, Catholics and Protestants and probably a few agnostics and atheists sitting side-by-side. Years ago in this town, this wouldn't be happening. Years ago, people in this area of Pennsylvania stayed with their own kind as if we were all afraid of catching a foreign disease from someone. But now at Linda's funeral, we see that this isn't so any longer. So what happened to Linda when she grew up? She married Nelson and together they created their own community of friends."

Linda's spirit smiles when she sees that Nancy is smiling and holding Nelson's hand.

"Some people may say Linda had a big heart. That's true. But I think she had an energetic heart. Her heart was filled with appreciation for the smallest and biggest things and people in her life. Give her a donut and she appreciated that chocolate donut as if it were a nugget of gold. Give her and Nelson a ride home from the bingo parlor and she appreciated both the vehicle and the driver as if she and her Babe were riding in a presidential motorcade. Make her laugh and she appreciated you as if you were a saint personified. She had the ability to forgive. A month before she died I was speaking with her on the telephone. She mentioned an incident that happened to her, a painful incident, when she was a child. I said to her, 'Oh, Linda, do you remember that?' She laughed and said, "Oh, Jooooooeeeeeyyyyyy, I remember everything." I asked her if that incident still bothered her, still hurt her, and she said 'Oh, Jooooeeeeeyyyyyy, nothing bothers me. I don't have time to be bothered about anything. I have Nelson now and he never bothers me.' She had the capacity to offer compassion to those who were less fortunate than herself. She never thought of herself as being better than anyone else, yet, she never demeaned herself and felt less worthy of love and friendship than anyone else. She was the epitome of humility and understanding. But she was also a champion of human rights, her rights and those of Nelson as human beings. She had a sense of justice, of valor, and she stood firm in retaining her innate sense of dignity. Oh, yes, she had a big heart, but more importantly, she had an energetic heart."

Holding the hand of the Angel of Eternal Memory, Linda's spirit smiles. She sees people gently and gracefully applauding.

"There is an ancient poem that says, 'The songs of the spheres in their revolution are what angels sing with their voices. As we are all children of Adam, each of us has faint memories of those celestial songs of paradise. But when we were born, earth and water covered our souls with their earthly veils, yet, we each retain memories of those heavenly voices. So the question is how shall you live your life dancing to the tune of the musical spheres?' Linda lived her life listening to the music within her heart, and her heart was beautiful, so therefore the music of heaven she is listening to at this moment must be extra-ordinarily beautiful, for so was she. And so, as we say 'goodbye' to Linda today, may I say to you Nelson, dear, dear Nelson, on behalf of Linda's ancestors, her grandparents and great-great grandparents, and her mother and father, and her brothers and sister, and her uncles and aunts and cousins, and to her wonderful friends throughout Greensburg, Pennsylvania, we owe both you and God one big thank you for being the answer to the question, "*What is going to happen to Linda when she grows up?*"

Everyone is standing at the realization it is time to accompany Linda's body to the cemetery. The shuffling of shoes, scraping of chairs, chattering words of support, condolences, and gratitude, are filling the heavy air as the mourners are following behind Nelson's wheelchair.

Exiting through the ornamented doors, tired and weary eyes are instantaneously focusing on the pink and white casket inside the polished hearse. Linda's body is beginning her final journey through her community within the Allegheny Mountains of western Pennsylvania, mountains serving as a reminder that despite death, life is a continuing process of assigned destiny.

The Angel of Eternal Memory's voice commands Linda to step out of the glass mirror. Meekly obeying, Linda's spirit is standing inside a multitude of spinning ice-crystal prisms which are forming human faces which are creating waves of white circular haloes. A brilliant bluish-white light disperses the faces which multiply as if rhythmically growing stronger by invisible blowing winds.

The Angel of Eternal Memory's voice speaks, "Only the ones with a beautiful heart can see the Light and hear the Sound of the Angels of Philokalias. You are one of the Angels of Philokalias, Linda. You always have been. You will abide and sing with them forever because you have attained this honor by the Light and Sound of your own beautiful heart as Linda Catherine Galata Heckman."

"I can't watch them take my body to the cemetery?"

"It's not necessary, Linda."

"What will happen to me now?"

"Forever your soul will be filled with the greatest of all joys, the joy of creating laughter, so that others on earth, those now there and those yet to come, may have the desire in their hearts to touch the finest threads of beauty."

Linda's spirit, illumined by a colorful mass of swirling atoms, swiftly transforms into her invisible but eternal translucent soul.

Flying through a mosaic of sparkling diamonds faces, each glorious countenance singing "I glorify life…. I rejoice in life… in the Essence of Delight, Beauty, Destiny, and Memory," Linda's joyful words echo throughout time and space…

"See you soon, Nelson!"

Photos

Linda and her brother Joey, the author of this book

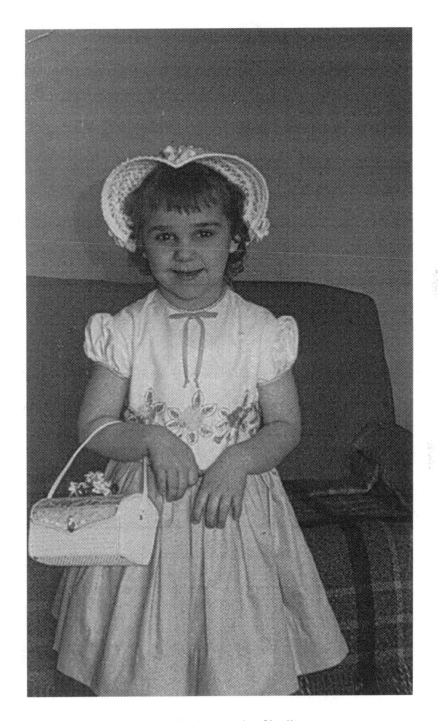

Her spirit had a touch of brilliance

#14   Her soul was as white as snow

In her heart was a little piece of heaven

Her laughter was all about love

Linda and Nelson, wife and husband for 33 years. They were an exceptional gift to one another.

Linda Catherine (Galata) Heckman, 54, of Greensburg died Wednesday, July 16, 2008 Excela Health Westmoreland Hospital, Greensburg. She was born April 24, 1954, in McKeesport, a daughter Jewel Slaney Galata and the late Joseph Galata. She is survived by her loving husband of 33 years Nelson; three brothers, Joseph, of Reno, Nev., David, of San Diego Calif., and Thomas, of Las Vegas Nev.; a sister, Nancy Boehm and her husband, Russell, of North Huntington; one brother-in-law two sisters-in-law; and severa aunts and uncles, nieces and nephews and cousins. A funera service was held in the funera home with Pastor Gene Stuckey officiating. Interment was in Penn Lincoln Memorial Park, North Huntingdon. Arrangements by the PANTALONE FUNERAL HOME INC., 409 W. Pittsburgh St., Greensburg, PA 15601, 724 837-0020 wwwpantalone.com Natale N. Pantalone, supervisor.

Linda's obituary

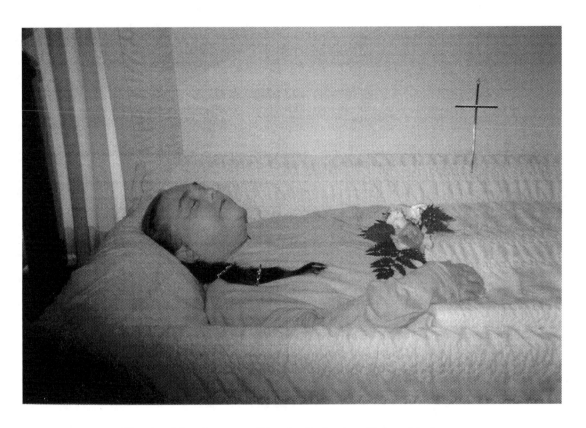

The deathless beauty of Linda Catherine Galata Heckman